Construction Trucks

Julie Murray

Abdo Kids Junior
is an Imprint of Abdo Kids
abdobooks.com

Abdo
TRUCKS AT WORK
Kids

abdobooks.com

Published by Abdo Kids, a division of ABDO, P.O. Box 398166, Minneapolis, Minnesota 55439.

Printed in the United States of America, North Mankato, Minnesota.

052023

092023

THIS BOOK CONTAINS
RECYCLED MATERIALS

Photo Credits: Getty Images, Shutterstock, ©Ditch Witch p.22/ CC BY 2.0

Production Contributors: Teddy Borth, Jennie Forsberg, Grace Hansen

Design Contributors: Candice Keimig, Pakou Moua

Library of Congress Control Number: 2022946716

Publisher's Cataloging-in-Publication Data

Names: Murray, Julie, author.

Title: Construction trucks / by Julie Murray

Description: Minneapolis, Minnesota : Abdo Kids, 2024 | Series: Trucks at work | Includes online resources and index.

Identifiers: ISBN 9781098266127 (lib. bdg.) | ISBN 9781098266820 (ebook) | ISBN 9781098267179 (Read-to-me ebook)

Subjects: LCSH: Trucks--Juvenile literature. | Vehicles--Juvenile literature. | Construction equipment--Juvenile literature.

Classification: DDC 388.32--dc23

Table of Contents

Construction Trucks

There are lots of construction trucks!

The dump truck carries

a big dirt load.

Liz drives the backhoe.

She digs a hole.

A boom truck has a **crane**.

It lifts heavy items.

A bulldozer helps move dirt and rocks.

A concrete mixer has a drum that spins. Concrete moves down the **chute**.

drum
chute

Gus drives a front loader.

He dumps the dirt.

A grader makes the dirt even.

140K

Have you seen any of these trucks?

More Construction Trucks

compactor

excavator

forklift

trencher

Glossary

chute
a passage down which things can slide.

crane
a machine with a tall arm that can move up and down or in a circle to lift and move heavy objects.

Index